Raw Ve   Desserts

Raw Food Ice Cream, Pudding, Cookie, Brownie, Candy, Cake, Pie and Cobbler Recipes.

By: Kevin Kerr

Copyright © 2015 by Kevin Kerr

All rights reserved.

Table of Contents

7 Raw Vegan Desserts

Introduction

Aside from tasting better, being better for your body, and being cruelty-free; uncooked vegan desserts take less prep time. Raw food is anything that isn't heated over 118 degrees so that the precious enzymes aren't destroyed. In order for food to digest it must be metabolized and broken down by enzymes. Science has recently discovered that our bodies can only produce so many enzymes in this lifetime which is the number one reason to eat as much raw food as you enjoy. The best way to start is by trying the desserts!

Chocolate Avocado Pudding

- 1 medium-sized avocado
- 3 tablespoons maple syrup
- 3 tablespoons raw cacao powder
- pinch of pink Himalayan salt

Blend until smooth and serve! Top with cacao nibs, goji berries, golden berries, mulberries, or hemp seeds.

Serves: 2.

Durian Ice Cream

- 1 pound durian
- 1 tablespoon maple syrup
- 3 drops peppermint oil
- 1 teaspoon spirulina
- ¼ cup cacao nibs
- ¼ cup hemp seeds or milled macadamia nuts

Blend or process the durian, honey, peppermint, and spirulina until smooth. Sprinkle on the toppings and enjoy your mint chocolate chip ice cream!

Serves: 1 to 3.

Orange Macadamia Pudding

- 2 peeled oranges
- 1 cup Macadamia nuts
- 1 cup dates
- 1-2 tablespoons liquefied coconut oil
- 1 teaspoon dried lavender flowers

Blend all the ingredients until smooth. If it is too thick, add the juice of another orange or two. Scoop into small, single serving dishes and leave in the fridge overnight.

Serves: 3 to 5.

Berry Pudding

- 1 banana
- handful frozen strawberries
- handful blueberries
- 3-5 pitted dates
- 1/4 teaspoon sea salt
- 1/2 teaspoon cinnamon
- 1/2 teaspoon vanilla
- 2 tablespoons cacao
- 1/4 cup non-dairy milk
- 1 tablespoon cashew butter

Blend and enjoy!

Serves: 2

Maple Ice Cream

- 2 frozen bananas
- 1-2 Tablespoons maple syrup
- 1/4 cup walnuts
- dash of cinnamon, to taste
- dash of nutmeg, to taste

Blend the bananas and maple syrup until smooth, in a food processor.

Add in the walnuts and spices, to taste. Blend and enjoy!

Serves: 1 or 2.

Brownies and Caramel Sauce

- 1 cup raw cacao powder
- 1 cup walnuts
- 1 cup pecans
- ¼ cup hemp seeds
- ¾ cup dried pitted dates
- 1 teaspoon maple syrup
- ¼ teaspoon sea salt

Using a food processor or high speed blender, mill and mix the ingredients until a thick batter-like consistency is reached. Put your brownie mix into a container, or form into individual treats. They are delicious without the sauce, but mixing the following ingredients in a blender will provide you with the perfect raw caramel sauce!

- 1 tablespoon raw cacao powder
- 1 teaspoon mesquite powder
- 1 teaspoon lucuma powder
- 4 teaspoons maple syrup
- 1 teaspoon organic maple syrup
- 1 teaspoon coconut oil

Blend well, top brownies, and enjoy!

Serves: 3 to 6.

Raw Chocolate Nut Butter Cookies

- 1 cup of your favorite raw nuts or seeds
- ½ cup of your favorite raw nut or seed butter
- ½ cup dried pitted dates
- 2 tablespoons raw cacao nibs
- 2 tablespoons maple syrup
- 2 tablespoons coconut oil

Blend or process all the ingredients until a cookie dough consistency is reached. Form into your desired shapes and refrigerate for at least one hour. Next, place the following ingredients in a bowl and dip each cookie.

- 3 tablespoons liquefied coconut oil
- 3 tablespoons raw cacao powder
- 2 tablespoons maple syrup

Serves: 2 to 4.

Raw Fig Cookies

- 2 pound raw figs
- 1 cup hemp seeds
- ½ cup macadamia nuts
- 2 tablespoons maple syrup
- ¼ teaspoon sea salt

First process or blend figs and set aside. Next, process or blend ½ cup hemp seeds, macadamia nuts, and salt. Add the rest of the hemp seeds, and mix together with a spoon. Form figs into desired shapes and cover with the milled nuts and seeds! ENJOY!

Serves: 4 to 10.

Chocolate Chip Cookies

- 1/2 cup raw organic Walnuts
- 1/2 cup raw organic Cashews
- 1 cup of your favorite variety of pitted dates
- 6 drops vanilla extract or ½ teaspoon dried vanilla bean powder
- 4 oz of your favorite organic chocolate bar
- 1 teaspoon of Maca powder

Blend or process all of the ingredients. A tablespoon of water be necessary depending on how dry the dates are.

Form into cookies, Enjoy!

Makes about 5 to 7 servings.

Oatmeal Raisin Cookies

- 2 cups raw organic oats
- 1 cup raw pecans
- 1/2 cup firmly packed grated fresh apple (about 2 medium apples)
- 1 cup dried raisins
- 1/2 cup pitted dates
- 4 Tbsp. organic liquefied coconut oil
- 3 tablespoons coconut sugar
- 1 teaspoon ground cinnamon
- 1/2 teaspoon ground ginger
- 1 teaspoon alcohol free vanilla extract
- 1 tablespoon freshly grated lemon zest
- pinch sea salt

Directions:

1. Add the pecans into a food processor fitted with the S blade, and a few times until roughly chopped. Empty them into a mixing bowl.
2. Place the oats in the food processor with the cinnamon, ginger, vanilla, sweetener, and sea salt and pulse a few times until well combined.
3. Add in the dates, apple, lemon zest, coconut oil and pulse again.
4. Transfer this mixture to a large bowl and fold through the remaining ingredients until a thick clustered "dough" forms.
5. Tweak the flavors to taste. You might want more sweetener, cinnamon or lemon zest.

6. Form this dough into medium sized cookies and place on mesh dehydrator sheets.
7. Dehydrate cookies in your dehydrator at 100 degrees for 12 - 15 hours or more depending on your preference.
8. This recipe yields 12 medium-sized dense chewy cookies. Alternatively, you could make 24 smaller cookies.

Note: For those of you without a dehydrator, you can try making these oatmeal cookies in a conventional oven by preheating your oven to 300 F, placing the cookies in, closing the oven door, turning the oven off and allowing it to cool with the cookies inside. The cookies should have a nice chewy texture.

Mulberry Kiwi Bars

- 1 1/2 cups dried mulberries
- 2 cups dried figs
- 2 cups pitted dates
- 2 tsp. of freshly ground cinnamon

Directions:

Place all ingredients in the food processor and pulse until the mixture reaches an even consistency. Take out the mixture, and press it into a glass bowl to form it. When ready, remove it and slice into bar chunks to make your energy bars. Now it's time to make the kiwi topping!

Ingredients for the Cherry Drizzle:

- 2 cups pitted cherries
- 1 cup pitted dates

Directions:

Blend both ingredients until desired consistency is reached! Dip energy bars in mixture and refrigerate for an hour! Enjoy!

Serves: 4

Chocolate Macadamia Nut Cookies

- 2 cups organic raw macadamia nuts
- 1/2 cup raw organic cacao powder
- 2 Tbsp. liquefied organic coconut oil
- 1/2 cup organic raw agave or maple syrup
- 2 tsp organic vanilla extract
- 1/2 tsp sea salt

Directions:

1. Place the macadamia nuts in the food processor and pulse a few times until coarsely ground.
2. Now add in the cacao powder and pulse a few times until the consistency of bread crumbs.
3. Add in all of the other ingredients and pulse until well combined. The mixture should form a ball.
4. Take this ball and roll it out to about a 1/4 inch on parchment paper.
5. Now cut out even small circles. I used the top of a shot glass.
6. Place these circles on dehydrator sheets and slowly warm at 115 degrees for 48 hours.
7. Store in a sealed container in the fridge for about 3 weeks.

Serves: 5

Gingerbread Cookies

- 2 cups of your favorite raw flour
- 1 1/2 cup pitted dates
- 1/8 teaspoon sea salt
- 1/2 teaspoon vanilla powder
- 2 Tablespoons fresh ginger
- 1 teaspoon cinnamon
- 1 teaspoon nutmeg
- 1 Tablespoon molasses
- 1/4 cup maple syrup
- 2 Tablespoons liquefied coconut oil

Directions:

Place all the ingredients in a food processor or blender and mix until even consistency is reached. Form into cookies and enjoy!

Serves 4 to 8.

Chocolate Pumpkin Brownies

- 1 Pie Pumpkin
- 2-3 Lbs. Pitted Dates
- 3 Ripe Persimmons
- Half Cup Raw Cacao Powder
- 1 Tbs Cinnamon
- 1 Cup raw organic Pecans
- 1 Cup Dried Black Mission Figs
- 1 Tbs. Pumpkin Spices (Nutmeg and Clove)
- 1 Thumbnail of Ginger
- 1 Small Vanilla Bean

Directions:

Add everything to your high speed blender and blend until even consistency is reached. Form into brownies and enjoy!

Serves 5 to 7.

Oreos

- 1/2 cup almonds
- 1/4 cup ground flax or chia
- 1/4 cup raw cacao powder
- 1/4 cup shredded coconut
- 1 Tablespoon maple syrup
- 1 teaspoon vanilla extract

For the stuffing:

- 1/4 cup cashews
- 2 Tablespoons shredded coconut
- 2 Tablespoons liquefied coconut oil
- 1 Tablespoon honey or maple syrup
- 1 teaspoon vanilla extract

Directions:

Blend the almonds and flax meal in a food processor until the almonds are a powder.

Add in the cacao, shredded coconut, sweetener and vanilla. Blend until the dough starts to stick together. You may need to add a splash of water.

You can either roll the dough out into a cylinder and cut the cookies that way or roll out the mixture and use a cookie cutter. I opted for the latter and used the lid from a bottle that was the perfect size. Make sure to have an even number of oreo halves at the end!

Place them in a dehydrator overnight or if you don't have one you can refrigerate.

Now it's time to do the filling! Blend up all of the ingredients in a food processor.

Sandwich the filling between the cookies and enjoy!

Serves: 4 to 6.

Chocolate Truffles

- 1 cup pitted dates
- 1/4 cup hemp hearts and a little extra for rolling truffles in
- 1 heaping Tablespoon of cacao powder and a little extra for rolling truffles in

Directions:

Blend the dates, hemp hearts and cacao in a food processor until the mixture sticks together. If your dates are super moist, you could even do this by hand in a bowl if you don't have a food processor.

Roll the mixture into balls.

Roll the truffles in some cacao powder, hemp hearts, leave them plain or all of the above!

Enjoy!

Serves: 2 to 4.

Almond Butter Cups

- 1/4 cup liquefied coconut oil
- 1/4 cup raw organic cacao powder
- 1 teaspoon maple syrup
- 2-3 Tablespoons almond butter

Directions:

Mix cacao powder and sweetener of choice in with coconut oil in a small bowl.

Fill 6 little paper cupcake cups with about a teaspoon of the chocolate in each.

Place in freezer for 5 minutes or until hardened.

Put a dollop of almond butter in each cup.

Cover with the remaining chocolate.

Freeze for another 5 minutes or until hardened.

Enjoy!

Serves: 3 to 4.

Real Chocolate

- 4 ounces raw organic cacao butter
- 3 ounces raw organic coconut oil
- 4 to 6 tablespoons raw organic cacao powder
- 2 teaspoons cinnamon
- Coconut sugar, lo han guo, goji berry, lucuma, maple syrup, cane sugar, stevia, schizandra berry, or yacon. You decide! I recommend lo han guo, stevia, or maple syrup for chocolate.

First, melt the cacao butter and coconut oil in your double-broiler system at the lowest temperature possible to save nutrients. Next, stir in the cacao powder, cinnamon and sweetener until you get a consistent "chocolate syrup". Pour into a plate or silicone molds and put into the refrigerator until it hardens up. It usually only takes an hour or less. Break into pieces or free from molds and enjoy! :)

Optional: If you want to get creative you can add dried fruits before you refrigerate such as dates, goji berries or mulberries. If you really want to make things interesting and healthy try adding nuts or seeds, nut butters, or superfood powders!

Chocolate Caramel Bars

- 2 cups raw almonds
- 1 1/2 cups pitted dates
- splash of vanilla extract

Caramel:

- 1 cup pitted dates
- 1 Tablespoon liquefied coconut oil
- 1/4 cup water
- splash of vanilla extract
- pinch of sea salt

Chocolate:

- 2 Tablespoons liquefied coconut oil
- 1/4 cup raw cacao powder
- 2 1/2 Tablespoons maple syrup
- pinch of sea salt

Directions:

Blend the almonds into a flour in your food processor.

Add in the dates and vanilla and blend until it sticks together.

Press this base mixture into a 9" x 9" pan, that's lined with parchment paper or cling wrap so that you can easily pull it out at the end to slice it.

Blend all of the caramel ingredients in your food processor until smooth and caramel-y. Add a splash more water if needed.

Spread the caramel on top of the base and place in the freezer while you mix up the chocolate.

Mix up all of the chocolate ingredients in a small bowl.

Spread the chocolate over the caramel.

Let the squares set in the freezer overnight.

Pull the squares out of the pan, slice them and ENJOY!

Serves: 4 to 6.

<u>Fudge</u>

- 2 pounds of pitted medjool dates
- 8 ounces of raw cashew butter

Blend together, form in a pan, cut into squares, top with goji or golden berries, and serve!

Fit for 3 to 5 people!

Lemon Coconut Bars

Base:

- 3/4 cup oats
- 3/4 cup dates
- 3/4 cup coconut shreds

Lemon layer:

- 1/3 cup melted coconut oil
- 1/4 cup maple syrup (or 1 cup dates, but this will change the color)
- Juice from 3 lemons
- 1/2 cup coconut shreds
- 1 or 2 bananas

To make the base: pulse the oats or buckwheat groats and coconut shreds in your food processor until they become rough flour. Add the dates and process until it all sticks together. Press into the bottom of a square baking pan and put in the fridge.

To make the lemon layer: blend all the ingredients until smooth. See if you like the taste and adjust accordingly. Spread evenly on to the base layer and set in the fridge overnight. The next day, cut into squares and sprinkle with finely ground coconut flakes and enjoy!

Serves: 5 to 7.

Raw Apple Apricot Cobbler

- 8 peeled and cored apples
- 4 sliced and quartered apricots
- ¼ cup organic maple syrup
- 3 tablespoons liquefied coconut oil
- 1 teaspoon cinnamon
- ¼ teaspoon sea salt

Mix all the ingredients except for the apricots in a blender or food processor until an even consistency is reached, then mix in the chunks of apricots but keep them whole. This will be used as the filling to this delicious dessert. Now it's time to make the shell and topping.

- 1 cup walnuts
- 1 cup dried pitted dates
- 3 tablespoons coconut oil
- 2 teaspoons cinnamon
- 1 ½ teaspoons vanilla extract or 1 vanilla bean

Mix the ingredients in a food processor or blender until an even chunky consistency is reached. Pour into a Pyrex pie crust but save enough for the topping. Top and serve! Fit for ten people. If you desire it warm you can heat at the lowest temperature possible in your oven or dehydrator for 20 minutes to several hours.

Serves: 4 to 6.

Watermelon Cake

- 1 watermelon
- 1 cup soaked hemp seeds
- 1 cup soaked cashews
- ½ cup coconut water
- 1 juiced lemon
- 2 vanilla beans
- 3 tablespoons raw honey
- ½ cup soaked almonds

Start by peeling the watermelon and shaping it to your desired size of cake(s). (Cup cakes are also possible.) Next, blend or process the rest of the ingredients until smooth. Cover the entire watermelon. Process the almonds and stick them to the sides of your cake. Top with your favorite fruits and refrigerate for an hour!

Serves: 3 to 6.

<u>Carrot Cake</u>

Macadamia Nut Frosting:
- 1 1/2 cups Macadamia Nuts
- Juice from 1 lemon
- 2 tablespoons liquefied coconut oil
- 2 tablespoons coconut sugar
- 1 teaspoon vanilla powder
- 1 tablespoon water

Carrot Cake:
- 3 large carrots, peeled and chopped into small chunks or pulp from 6 large carrots that were juiced
- 1 1/2 cups oats
- 2 cups pitted dates
- 1/2 cup dried coconut powder
- 1 teaspoon cinnamon
- 1/2 teaspoon nutmeg

Frosting:

Blend all ingredients in your high speed blender until smooth, adding water as needed. Put in the fridge for at least an hour before using.

Cake:

Process the oats into flour in your food processor then add the rest of the ingredients in and process until it begins to stick together. Put the mixture into a bowl to form it into your cake or simply construct it into your desired shape then put in the freezer until it's solid. Then simply frost your cake and you officially have the healthiest and most delicious carrot cake in the world! Enjoy!

Serves: 3 to 4.

Vanilla Cheesecake

Crust:

- 1 cup pitted medjool dates
- 2 cups raw almonds

Surround the inside of a cake pan with wax paper or plastic wrap. Pulse dates and nuts together in food processor until you get an even consistency. Form and press mixture into the bottom of the pan. Put in fridge for at least and hour before putting the cake together.

Cheesecake:

- 3 cups soaked raw cashews
- 3/4 cup lemon juice
- 2/3 cup maple syrup
- 3/4 cup liquefied coconut oil
- 1/2 teaspoon sea salt
- 1 teaspoon vanilla extract
- 1 vanilla bean

Blend all ingredients, except coconut oil, together until smooth and creamy. Add coconut oil and make sure it blends completely. Pour onto crust in cake pan and set in the fridge for at least two hours. Take out of cake pan holding onto the wax paper or plastic wrap and put it on a plate.

Slice and enjoy!

Serves: 2 to 6.

Cinnamon Cake

Dough:

- 1 cup pecans
- 1/2 cup ground flax seed
- 1/4 cup maple syrup
- 3 tablespoons raw buckwheat flour
- 5 pitted dates

Filling:

- 1/2 cup pitted medjool dates
- 1/4 cup water
- 2 tablespoons cinnamon
- 1 tablespoon liquefied coconut oil
- 1/4 teaspoon sea salt
- 4 pitted medjool dates
- 2 tablespoons chopped hazelnuts

Icing:

- 1 cup cashews
- 1/4 cup coconut oil
- 4 tablespoons fresh squeezed lemon juice
- 1 tablespoon maple syrup

Directions

- Mix all of the dough ingredients in a food processor until it starts sticking together until it forms a dough. Set aside.
- Mix all of the filling ingredients in a food processor or a blender until well blended.

- In a medium sized spring form pan or form your cake to the desired shape you want with your hands.
- Put in the freezer for about an hour to make it easier to apply icing.
- Mix all of the icing ingredients in a food processor or blend together until desired consistency is reached.
- Ice the cake!
- Top with cinnamon and your favorite chopped nuts.

Enjoy!

Serves: 4 to 7.

Mini Chocolate Cake

Crust:

- 1/3 cup pecans
- 1/3 cup pitted medjool dates
- 2 teaspoons cacao powder

Filling:

- 1 avocado
- 1 tablespoon cacao powder
- 1 tablespoon maple syrup

Chocolate topping:

- 2 tablespoons liquefied coconut oil
- 2 tablespoons cacao powder
- 1 teaspoon maple syrup, or to taste.

Directions:

Blend the crust ingredients, using a food processor, and press the mixture down into a spring form cake pan.

Blend the filling ingredients, using a food processor, and spoon the mixture on top of the crust in the spring form pan.

Place the torte in the freezer while you make the chocolate topping.

Mix the chocolate ingredients in a small bowl.

Pour the chocolate sauce over top of the torte.

Freeze overnight and enjoy!

Serves: 1 or 2.

Coconut Cream Pie

Crust:
- 1 1/2 cups nuts
- 1 1/2 cups pitted medjool dates
- pinch of sea salt

Chocolate Cream:
- 2 avocados
- 1/3 cup maple syrup
- 1/2 teaspoon cinnamon
- 1/4 cup raw cacao powder
- 2 tablespoon mesquite powder
- 2 tablespoons liquefied coconut oil
- pinch of sea salt

Whipped Cream:
- 1 ½ cups of coconut milk
- 3 tablespoons raw coconut sugar
- 1 vanilla bean

Crust:

Pulse nuts in food processor until they're the size of crumbs. Add dates and pulse until it lumps together. Feel free to add cinnamon, salt, vanilla or more sweetener here. Press into your favorite pie pan and stick in the fridge.

Chocolate Cream:

Blend or process all ingredients until silky smooth. Now slice 3-4 bananas and put them on the bottom of the crust. Spoon on the chocolate cream and put on another player of banana slices. Set in the fridge again.

Right before serving, take out coconut milk from the fridge. Spoon off the thick fat from the top - you want this. Put the milk you spooned out into a mixing bowl with the sugar and beat until it turns into a cream! Spoon over your pie and enjoy!

Serves: 3 to 4.

Raw Pumpkin Pie

Crust:

- 1 cup cashews
- 1 cup almonds
- 1/4 cup pitted medjool dates
- 1 cup dates
- 1/8 teaspoon sea salt

Pumpkin Filling:

- 1 cubed pie pumpkin without the seeds
- 1 cup dates
- 4-5 tablespoons liquefied coconut oil
- 1/3 cup maple syrup
- 1-4 tablespoons pumpkin pie spice (cinnamon, nutmeg, ginger and cloves)

Crust:

Process the nuts in your food processor until they are like a rough flour. Add the dates, raisins and salt. Pulse until it all sticks together in a lump. Press into the bottom of a pie dish and refrigerate.

Pie Filling:

Process the pumpkin cubes until they can't get any smaller in your food processor. Add in the other ingredients and process until it can't get any smoother. Transfer the filling to your high speed blender and blend on the highest setting until an even consistency is reached. Spread the filling onto your pie crust and let it set in the fridge for a few hours.

Serves: 3 to 6.

Citrus Coconut Cheesecake

Crust:
- 1 cup walnuts
- 1 cup almonds
- 1 cup pitted medjool dates

Lemon Layer:
- 3 cups cashews
- 1 cup coconut milk
- juice of 2 lemons
- 3 tablespoons maple syrup
- 1/2 teaspoon sea salt
- 3 tablespoons liquified coconut oil

Lime Layer:
- 1 avocado
- juice of 2 limes
- 3 tablespoons maple syrup
- 1 tablespoon coconut oil
- 1/8 cup coconut milk
- 1/4 cup coconut flakes

Crust:

Blend all the ingredients in your food processor until it starts clumping together so you can press it into shapes. Press into the bottom of a spring form pan lined with plastic wrap. Put in fridge for at least an hour.

Lemon Layer:

Blend all ingredients together in your blender until creamy smooth. Pour half of it onto your crust and set aside the remaining half. Put back in the fridge for another hour.

Lime Layer:

Blend all ingredients until smooth in your food processor or blender. Tour all of this onto the first layer on the crust, and then pour on the remaining lemon layer from earlier. Let it sit in the fridge for at least a few hours. Enjoy!

Serves: 4 to 6.

<u>Chia Fruit Pie</u>

Crust:

- 1/4 cup pitted medjool dates
- 1/4 cup raisins
- 1/4 cup dried figs

Filling:
- 2 bananas
- 2 tablespoon chia or flax seeds

Topping:
- 3/4 cup chopped strawberries
- 3/4 cup chopped kiwi
- 1 medium-sized mango

To make the crust:

Put all the ingredients in your food processor and pulse until everything is in small pieces that stick together - don't process too much or it will be hard to work with. Press into an aluminum pie tin. Put in the fridge.

To make the filling:

Mash the banana with fork and then add the chia or flax seeds.

Assembly:

Take the crusts gently out of the tins. Spread the banana chia mix into the crusts and then top off with the fruit. Enjoy!

Serves: 3 to 4.

Made in the USA
Las Vegas, NV
04 April 2022